Amazing Birds

Coloring Book

Ruth Soffer

Dover Publications, Inc., Mineola, New York

Introduction

To us poor unfeathered beings, even the most common birds, fluttering and twittering in the avian traffic jam around the backyard feeder or waking us with their sweet chorus on summer mornings, are amazing creatures. But the ones you will meet in this book are the champs.

Here you will meet the most talented singers (the red-and-yellow barbet and the northern mockingbird) and the most persuasive talkers (the hill mynah, the African gray parrot, and the raven). You will meet birds with spectacular mating displays, such as the lilac-breasted roller and the great frigatebird, and others that attract their mates through their exquisite plumage, such as the long-tailed widowbird, the bird of paradise, and the mandarin duck. You will also see birds with unusual nesting habits: the cuckoo, which lays its eggs in other birds' nests; the hornbill, which seals itself inside a tree for almost two months; the emperor penguin, whose egg rests atop its father's feet till it hatches; and the masked weaver, whose nest is an onion-shaped architectural masterpiece.

Copyright

Copyright © 2006 by Ruth Soffer
All rights reserved.

Bibliographical Note

Amazing Birds Coloring Book is a new work, first published
by Dover Publications, Inc., in 2006.

International Standard Book Number

ISBN-13: 978-0-486-44796-4
ISBN-10: 0-486-44796-0

Manufactured in the United States by Courier Corporation
44796004   2015
www.doverpublications.com

The **red-and-yellow barbets** (*Trachyphonus erythrocephalus*) of East Africa are famous for singing in harmony. They live in groups of three to six birds, but usually only the main male and female sing a duet—occasionally joined briefly by others. Barbets often dig their nests in termite mounds. They have a yellow face and front, red cheeks and throat, and white-spotted black wings. The female (to the right) has a red crown with black spots. The male has an all-black crown with a slight crest.

Lilac-breasted rollers *(Coracias caudata)*, which are widespread in the middle of Africa, get their name from the amazing stunts the males do to attract a mate. They dive and roll and twist in the sky like flashes of light. These birds, which are about fourteen inches long, prey on lizards and invertebrates, but sometimes also take small birds. These rollers are gorgeously colored. Their wings and tails are colored bright blue, buff, and teal. Their bellies are teal, their throats rust or lilac, and their heads and faces buff or greenish.

In November, male **long-tailed widowbirds** (*Euplectes progne*), which also live in the middle of Africa, begin to change they way they look. Their feathers change from brown to glossy black, and their tails lengthen tremendously. A bird the size of a house sparrow can have a tail twenty inches long. At this season the males are black with a white splotch, and a smaller splotch of red, on the shoulders. At the end of the breeding season, the males lose their long tail feathers and become streaky brown, like the females.

Raggiana birds of paradise (*Paradisaea raggiana*), found in New Guinea, are among the most beautiful birds in the world. To attract a mate the male goes into the treetops with three to eight other males, and they all screech and display for the females. If a female sits down next to one of the males, he leans forward till he hangs almost upside down and fans out his feathers and tail plumes. After breeding, the female does all the nest building and incubation. Her drab brown colors camouflage her on the nest. The male has red plumes, reddish-brown body feathers, an emerald-green throat, a yellow head, and a blue beak.

The **great gray owl** (*Strix nebulosa*) is the largest owl in North America and one of the largest in the world. It can be thirty-three inches long and may have a wingspan of five feet. The great grays live in coniferous northern forests and hunt equally well in day and night. They live on voles and other small rodents and birds. They are dusky gray, with yellow eyes, a black spot on the chin, and a dark ruff, containing concentric circles of gray-brown on white, around the face. Their call is a deep, booming whoo-hoo-hoo.

Ravens (*Corvus corax*) and their smaller cousins (such as crows, jays, and magpies) are noted for their intelligence. They are playful and adaptable, changing their behavior to solve new problems. They often imitate the sounds of other birds, animals, humans—even an alarm clock. Ravens are fairly large, about the size of a hawk, and are a glossy blue-black. They live throughout most of North Amercia, Asia, much of Europe, and North Africa.

Some people in East Asia use the **great cormorant** (*Phalacrocorax carbo*) to bring them their dinner. They tie the birds to their boats with long strings so the cormorants can hunt for fish underwater, but they put rings around the birds' necks so they can't swallow the fish. The great cormorant is the largest and most widespread member of the cormorant family. It can be found in North America, Europe, Africa, and Australia, as well as Asia. Adult great cormorants are black, with a white throat and a yellow chin pouch. The bill is gray and the legs and feet are black.

Hill mynahs *(Gracula religiosa)* of Southeast Asia are able to mimic human speech with uncanny accuracy. They can do so much better than any parrot, with perfect enunciation and sometimes extensive vocabularies. Sometimes they even seem to understand what they're saying. These birds are glossy black with a white band across each wing and yellow areas from beneath the eyes to the back of the head. Their beaks look like candy corn—bright orange with yellow at the tip.

The **mandarin duck** (*Aix galericulata*) is one of the most beautiful birds in the world. The male has an olive-brown back and tail, with a striking pair of orange "sail" feathers rising from his back. He has a crest of orange and cream feathers, a broad white eye stripe, and a reddish face and whiskers. His breast is maroon with black and white vertical stripes, and his abdomen and underside are white with gold and black flanks. His bill is red, his legs whitish, and his feet yellow. The female is duller in color—mostly gray, with a curving white stripe behind the eye—and has no sail feathers. Mandarin ducks live in East Asia. Because males and females stay together for several seasons, they are regarded in China and Japan as a symbol of love and marital fidelity.

The **great frigatebird** (*Fregata minor*), found from the western Atlantic through the Pacific and Indian Oceans, is a fine flyer with a seven-foot wingspan. But it is best known for its spectacular courting behavior. The males are mostly black with orange throats, but at mating season their throat pouches become bright red. The males sit quietly in the low shrubs waiting for a female to fly overhead. When that happens, the males puff air into their pouches till they look like red balloons, and they wag their heads from side to side, clap their bills, and wave their wings wildly to attract the female. If the display is convincing enough, the female will land and sit beside some lucky male.

The **common kingfisher** (*Alcedo atthis*) lives near rivers throughout Europe, except in northern areas where the rivers freeze, and also North Africa and Asia. It lives in long tunnels that it has dug in the river bank, and it dives deep into the river to catch fish. When a kingfisher has caught a fish he beats it against a branch to kill it before swallowing it. At mating time, males offer females a fish they have caught. Kingfishers are blue, with a rust-orange breast and cheeks, white throat, and a short white collar.

11

Like the American cowbird, the **European cuckoo** (*Cuculus canorus*) gets other birds to raise its young. The female pushes one of the eggs out of another bird's nest and lays her own in its place. The cuckoo egg hatches sooner than the others in the nest, and the baby cuckoo pushes the other eggs out of the nest. The foster mother doesn't seem to notice, and raises the young cuckoo as her own—even though it may be twice her size. The European cuckoo is found throughout Europe and east to India. Cuckoos are gray, with dark backs and light undersides.

The **great hornbill** *(Buceros bicornis)* of India and Southeast Asia is unusual in its nesting habits. The female seals herself inside the hollow of a tree with dung and mud (with her mate helping from the outside) and stays there for six or eight weeks, until her young are almost ready to leave the nest. She leaves only a narrow slit so the male can bring her food. Her diet consists mostly of fruit. Hornbills mate for life. They are dressed in black plumage, with a white neck, white wing bars, and a white tail crossed with a black bar. They have a huge yellow bill with a yellow "casque" on top.

In a single day, a **European bee-eater** (*Merops apiaster*) may eat as many as 250 bees, wasps, hornets, and other insects. It catches them in midair, but before eating them it removes the sting by repeatedly hitting the insects on a hard surface. These bee-eaters breed in southern Europe and in parts of north Africa and western Asia. They nest communally in sandy banks near river shores, making long tunnels for their eggs. The bee-eater is richly colored. It has a brown back, turning yellow near the wings. The wings and breast and eyebrow are teal green, the forehead is white, and the throat is bright yellow. The bird in the foreground is fluffing its feathers to warm them in the sun.

Most herons fly away when frightened, but the **American bittern** *(Botaurus lentiginosus)* stays put and disguises itself. It stretches its neck up, points its bill towards the sky, and sways slowly from side to side, blending in with the reeds moving in the breeze. If this doesn't fool the intruder, the bittern will fly off with a low barking call. The bittern's back is brown with black speckles, and it has a long dark patch extending from below the eye down the side of the neck. Its underside is streaked brown and white. American bitterns live in marshy areas throughout North America except in the far north.

The **emperor penguin** *(Aptenodytes forsteri)* is the largest penguin, standing about four feet tall. It breeds during the long darkness of the Antarctic winter. In April or May, emperors gather at rookeries as far as sixty or seventy miles inland. Within a few hours after the female lays her single egg, the male places it on top of his feet and covers it with a warm fold of skin. While he stands around waiting for the egg to hatch, the female travels back to the open sea to feed on fish and squid. About two months later she will return to raise and feed the newly hatched chick. The emperor penguin has a black back and a white front, a yellow patch of feathers behind the eyes, and a black bill with a yellow-orange streak.

With its bright blue face, red eyes, and spiky orange hairdo, the **hoatzin** (*Opisthocomus hoazin*), which lives in swamps of the Amazon and Orinoco basins of South America, looks like a chicken from outer space. It eats mostly leaves and has a special foregut, like that of a cow, that allows it to break down plant fiber into sugars. Another peculiarity of the hoatzin is that its nestlings have two little claws on each wing, which help them to hold onto branches and clamber back into the nest if they fall out. The hoatzin has chestnut-brown feathers, with a buff-colored throat and breast. It has a long, bronze-green tail ending in white.

What is unusual about the **brown pelican** (*Pelecanus occidentalis*) is the large pouch of skin it has in its long gray bill. This pouch holds more than twice what its stomach can hold—almost three gallons! To catch fish, the pelican drops from the air with wings partly folded, dives into the water, and uses this pouch as a net. It scoops up fish and water, strains out the water from the corner of its mouth, tips back its head, and swallows the fish. Brown pelicans can be found on the Atlantic, Pacific, and Gulf coasts from the United States down to Venezuela and Chile. They are about four feet long, with a gray-brown body, white head and neck, pale yellow crown, pale yellow eyes, grayish bill, and black legs and feet.

The **harpy eagle** (*Harpia harpyja*) is one of the most powerful eagles in the world. It can have a seven-foot wingspan, can weigh up to twenty pounds, and can have talons the size of grizzly-bear claws. The female may be as much as twice as heavy as her mate. Harpy eagles are found in Central and South America, but have become critically endangered. They feed primarily on animals that live in the trees, like sloths, monkeys, opossums, and some reptiles and birds. The back of the harpy eagle is slate black, and its underside is white with a black band across the chest. The head is pale gray and crowned with a double crest.

No other animal is as adept in copying songs and sounds from its environment as the **northern mockingbird** *(Mimus polyglottos)*. A single bird may have a repertoire of 50 to 200 sounds—including not only the songs of other birds, but the sounds of frogs, crickets, squirrels, barking dogs, and even bells, piano notes, and the squeaking of a rusty gate! The northern mockingbird ranges from southern Canada to Mexico. It has a gray body and head, white under parts, and a long black tail with white outer tail feathers. It has a white wing patch, black legs, and yellow eyes.

The **blue-footed booby** (*Sula nebouxii*), found along the Pacific coast from Peru to Mexico, is best known for its bright blue feet and clownish look. But it's a very skilful fisherman. It glides over the water, and when it sees a fish it can dive from eighty feet in the air and streak into the water with hardly a splash. Blue-footed boobies nest in colonies. To impress his lady, the male parades in front of her, raising his blue feet one at a time for her approval. Both the male and the female stretch their necks and point their bills to the sky, and the male spreads his wings and whistles. The blue-footed booby has a white chest and underside, brown wings and tail, and a brown streaked head. Its beak is dark gray.

The **wandering albatross** (*Diomedea exulans*), which soars above the southern oceans, is the largest of sea birds and has the largest wingspan of any bird. Its wingspan can reach more than eleven feet. It is a powerful flier. In the past, these majestic birds often accompanied sailing ships for days, even in stormy weather. They feed on squid, small fish, and animal refuse, and sleep on the surface of the water. At breeding time they retire to islands where they nest in a natural hollow or a circle of earth scraped together on the open ground. These birds are mostly white, with brownish black wingtips and wing edges and pinkish bills.

The **greater roadrunner** *(Geococcyx californianus),* which can run twenty miles an hour, feeds on insects, scorpions, lizards, mice, other birds, and snakes. Because of its lightning quickness, it is one of the few animals that can prey on rattlesnakes. It grabs the rattler by the tail, cracks it like a whip, and dashes it against the ground till it's dead. The roadrunner swallows its prey whole. If a snake is too long to be swallowed completely, its tail dangles from the roadrunner's mouth until enough of the snake is digested for it to swallow some more. The roadrunner has a mottled brown and white back, a mostly white breast, a white patch behind its yellow eyes, and a long, white-tipped tail.

The **ostrich** (*Struthio camelus*) is the largest bird in the world. It may weigh as much as 300 pounds and stand more than eight feet tall. Ostriches can not fly, but can run thirty miles an hour. Contrary to common belief, they do not bury their heads in the sand. If a female is threatened while sitting on her nest, she may press her neck flat, blending with the background. The male ostrich has glossy black body feathers and white wings and tail feathers. Females and young males are grayish brown. Both males and females have bare necks and thighs, showing skin that is blue or pink in males and pinkish gray in females. Ostriches live in Africa and eat shoots, leaves, flowers, and seeds.

The **African gray parrot** *(Psittacus erithacus)* is intelligent and sensitive, and may be the best talker of all the birds. It easily learns hundreds of words and other sounds. Recent studies show that African grays can actually understand the meanings of some words. African gray parrots have been kept as pets since Roman times. In the wild, they live in large flocks in western and central Africa. They may live as long as fifty to sixty-five years. They have gray feathers, white patches around the eyes, and red tail feathers. Their curved bill is dark gray.

25

The **Andean condor** (*Vultur gryphus*) is the largest bird of prey in the world, with a wingspan of about ten feet and a weight of twenty to thirty pounds. Their huge wings allow them to soar almost indefinitely on rising air currents high over the mountains of South America. Their usual food is dead, dying, or sometimes newborn animals. The Andean condor is black with white patches on the wings and a downy white ruff around the neck. Its head and neck are naked, with reddish-black skin hanging in loose folds. Males have a fleshy comb over the beak. Males' eyes are brown, and females' are garnet red. These condors have been known to live more than 70 years in captivity.

Hoopoes (*Upupa epops*), which range across Eurasia and Africa, have an unusual way of dealing with threats. When it is in the air, a hoopoe can fly away from a bird of prey. But if it is threatened while on the ground, it seems to play dead: It flattens itself on the ground, spreads its tail and wings, and throws its head back with its bill straight up. The hoopoe spends much of its time on the ground searching for insects, spiders, centipedes, and earthworms to eat. It is an exotic-looking bird with a pinkish-brown body, striking black-and-white wings, a long black down-curved bill, and a long pinkish-brown crest, which it raises when excited.

The **peregrine falcon** (*Falco peregrinus*) is the fastest bird in the world. It may reach a speed of 200 miles per hour when diving for prey. In the 1950s and 1960s peregrines were almost wiped out by the insecticide DDT. But now they have made a comeback and are among the most widespread birds in the world. They are found on all continents except Antarctica. The peregrine is slate-gray above, with a pale throat and breast. It has a black cap and "mustache" and has black and white bars on its belly and under wings.

The **bee hummingbird** (*Mellisuga helenae*), found in Cuba, is not only the smallest of all birds, but the world's smallest warm-blooded vertebrate. It weighs less than a penny and is less than two inches from tip to tail. When flying, its wings beat eighty times per second. It eats half its weight and drinks eight times its weight every day. The bee hummingbird has a bluish green body. In females and non-breeding males, the underside is pale gray. Breeding males are much more spectacular, with a pink to fiery red head, chin, and throat.

The **masked weaver** *(Ploceus velatus)*, which lives in Africa, is known for its well-made nests. The male weaves blades of grass or strips of palm leaf into a wonderful onion-shaped nest for his mate. If she likes it she'll move in and line the inside with grass seeds and feathers. These birds are mostly yellow, with a distinctive black facial mask, and streaked, yellowish green upper parts.